Phillis Wheatley
Poet

Written by Garnet Nelson Jackson
Illustrated by Cheryl Hanna

MODERN CURRICULUM PRESS

Program Reviewers

MODERN CURRICULUM PRESS
13900 Prospect Road, Cleveland, Ohio 44136
Simon & Schuster • A Paramount Communications Company

Copyright © 1993 Modern Curriculum Press, Inc.

Library of Congress Cataloging-in-Publication Data

Jackson, Garnet
    Phillis Wheatley, poet/written by Garnet Nelson Jackson; illustrated by Cheryl Hanna.
    p. cm. — (Beginning biographies)
    Summary: A brief biography of the enslaved African who learned to read and write, became the second woman in America to have a book published, and won international fame for her poetry.
    1. Wheatley, Phillis, 1753-1784 —Biography — Juvenile literature. 2. African American poets — 18th century — Biography — Juvenile literature. 3. Slaves — United States — Biography — Juvenile literature [1. Wheatley, Phillis, 1753-1784. 2. Poets, American. 3. Slaves. 4. African Americans — Biography.] I. Hanna, Cheryl, ill. II. Title. III. Series: Jackson, Garnet. Beginning biographies.
PS866.W5Z62 1993 811'.1 — dc20 [B] 92-28778 CIP AC
ISBN 0-8136-5233-2 (Reinforced Binding)   ISBN 0-8136-5706-7 (Paperback)

10 9 8 7 6 5 4 3 2 1   97 96 95 94 93

Text Printed on Recycled Paper

A sunbeam fell across the face of a little girl sleeping in her home in West Africa. The sunbeam gave bright colors to her dreams just before her eyes opened.

Fatou rose and twirled happily in the sun's rays, as she did every morning. Through the window, she saw her mother stretch out on the dew-covered grass. This was a Muslim way of greeting the new day.

3

4

Later, as Fatou and her friends
played outside their village, she ran
off too far. Suddenly she was
grabbed and dragged far from her
village. She was kidnapped !

Fatou spent many days in the bottom of an awful ship. It carried its load of kidnapped children and grown-ups across the Atlantic Ocean to America. In those long-ago days, some African people were sold in America as slaves. Slaves had to work for their owners all their lives without pay.

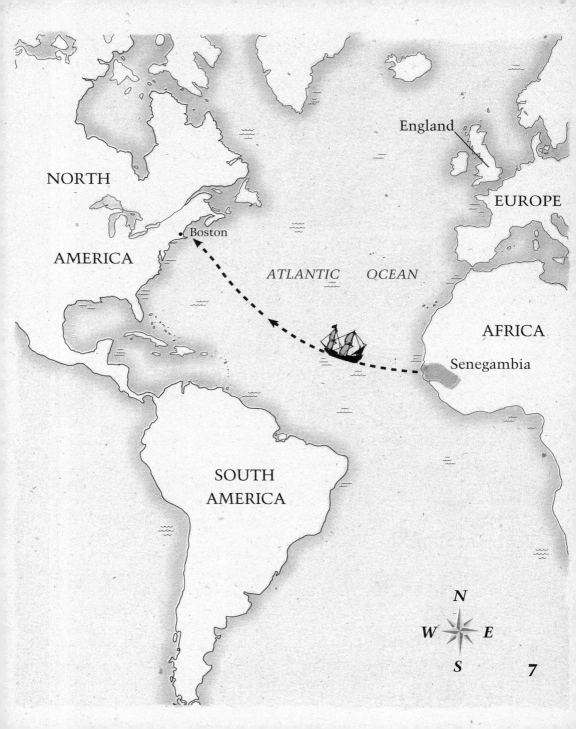

NORTH

AMERICA

Boston

ENGLAND

EUROPE

ATLANTIC   OCEAN

AFRICA

Senegambia

SOUTH
AMERICA

N

W   E

S

7

Fatou was taken from the ship to the slave market in the city of Boston. There Mrs. Susannah Wheatley bought Fatou to be her slave girl. She changed Fatou's name to "Phillis."

Phillis learned English quickly. Mrs. Wheatley saw how smart Phillis was. She allowed her own teen-aged children, Mary and Nat, to teach Phillis to read. Soon Phillis taught herself to write.

Learning how to read and write made Phillis different because most slaves were not allowed to do these things. Many slave-owners did not want slaves to know very much. But the Wheatleys allowed Phillis to read their books and gave her paper and pens for writing.

Although Phillis was treated kindly by her new family, the scary adventures of her past often made her sad.

At times she felt very
lonely in her
new home.

But she liked reading and learning.
Writing, in particular, always made
her smile. She loved to write
poems.

When Phillis wrote, she shared her
ideas and wishes. She visited
places she could have only
dreamed of. She was able to
invent places and make them what
she wanted them to be.

NORTH

AMERICA

Boston

ATLANTIC OCEAN

England

EUROPE

AFRICA

Senegambia

N

W   E

S

As Phillis grew up, she wrote more and more beautiful poems. When she was only 15, she wrote a poem to the King of England!

Two years later, the first collection of her poetry was published in America. She was becoming a famous poet.

A few years later, Phillis visited England. There, lords and ladies wanted to meet the young woman who wrote so beautifully.

When a complete book of her poems was published in England, Phillis became the second American woman to have a book published.

After she returned to America, Phillis was freed. She met a wonderful man, fell in love, and married.

23

Even though she lived nearly 200 years ago, Phillis Wheatley is remembered today as one of America's important poets.

Glossary

colony (käl´ ə nē) *plural* **colonies** A group of people who live in one country but are ruled by another country from which they came

Fatou (fa tu´) A person's name from Senegal, Africa, which means "brilliant"; it may have been Phillis Wheatley's African name.

lady (lād´ ē) *plural* **ladies** 1. A woman, especially a polite woman. 2. A special title for a woman who belongs to an important family.

lord (lôrd) A person with power, a master

Muslim (muz´ lim *or* mooz´ lim) A word describing people or things that are part of the religion of Islam

Senegambia (sen´ i gam´ bē a) A country in west Africa that no longer exists; it was made up of lands that are in the modern countries of Senegal and Gambia.